Barbaro

Beyond Brokenness

Library of Congress Cataloging-in-Publication Data

Names: Lifshin, Lyn, author.
Title: Barbaro : beyond brokenness : poems / Lyn Lifshin.
Description: Second edition. | Huntsville, Texas : TRP: The University
Press of SHSU, [2022]
Identifiers: LCCN 2022010855 (print) | LCCN 2022010856 (ebook) | ISBN
9781680032871 (paperback) | ISBN 9781680033007 (ebook) p
Subjects: LCSH: Barbaro (Race horse)--Poetry. | Race horses--Poetry. |
LCGFT: Poetry.
Classification: LCC PS3562.I4537 B37 2022 (print) | LCC PS3562.I4537
(ebook) | DDC 811/.54--dc23/eng/20220420
LC record available at https://lccn.loc.gov/2022010855
LC ebook record available at https://lccn.loc.gov/2022010856

SECOND EDITION
Cover and Interior design by Miranda Ramírez
Cover Image: CANVA Stock Vector
Printed and bound in the United States of America
First Edition Copyright: 2009

Published by TRP: The University Press of SHSU
Huntsville, Texas 77341
texasreviewpress.org

Barbaro

Beyond Brokenness

Lyn Lifshin

TRP: The University Press of SHSU
Huntsville, Texas

Table of Contents

You Need a Miracle to Get Through This (July)

Barbaro in the Light, Glistening and Dripping (August)

Against All Odds (September, October)

Beyond Us (November)

Why Do These Horses Mean So Much? (December)

The Final Miracle, Fiction (January)

Beyond Pain (Barbaro's Death)

The Sad Songs Haunt the Longest (Barbaro: Beyond Brokenness)

A Scoop of Vanilla Ice Cream on His Forehead
(Barbaro's Early Years)

April 29, 2002

I want to see the barn
the night Barbaro was born,
dark with a pale glow.
I want a video of the
nose, then the head
with stars on sweet
hay, want his first
sound. Give me the
blood sound as he is
pulled from La Ville,
the drops on straw,
rubies as Barbaro
wobbles to his feet,
a big bay colt trailing
bits of his mother.
I want a sketch of his
long legs like stilts
on the hay as his mare
licks him. And what
of those sounds of
night birds in stillness,
his bewilderment at
this new world

When I Think of Barbaro's Birth

of the foaling men
kneeling in golden
straw, his mare's
mid section heaving.
La Ville Rouge's
coat glistening with
sweat. I think of her
eyes rolling, her
groans and the men
each taking a foot,
the mare's nostrils

flaring. Night, a wind
of straw, manure,
sweat, dust, urine and
the night's cool air.
How they must have
wondered at the bay
colt's size as Barbaro's
wet and bloody head,
shoulders, torso and
black legs slid from
the mare. Down the
road, a truck backfires.
Flat on her side, La
Ville Rouge lifts her
head, looks at her new
born colt sprawled on
the soaked straw,
eyes blinking, a scoop
of vanilla ice cream on
his forehead. I imagine
La Ville Rouge
struggling to her feet,
neighing softly to her
baby and licking him,
how Barbaro tries to
stand up, spills, his legs
rubbery, falling back into
the straw until suddenly
he stands, swaying like
a willow, takes a step,
jerky, hardly graceful
but the starting point for
an unknown journey

Feathers Cushioning Barbaro's Hooves Inside the Mother's Body

Bill Sanborn

In the few seconds
after Barbaro was born
one man remembers
thinking "Lotta leg,"

says "you know if you
like a horse or don't.
The first time I saw him
was on a fourteen day

pregnancy scan on
ultra sound. I knew
him since he was a follicle."

As Barbaro Twisted Toward His Mother's Milk

the cord that held them
broke, dangled between
them. Later, they would
not recognize each
other, would always be
separate. But for this
April the colt shivers,
his first night, sticks
out his tongue and when
sun comes thru the barn
window, smells the
hay and straw, warm
milk, moves out into the
sound of birds under
the trees in the
braid of his mother

On That First Morning

the Kentucky pasture
looked blue. You
could imagine grass
washed with a brush
to match the sky.
Another foal could
smell how his scent
of mare's milk,
nuzzled the white
on his front feet.
It was as if the
radish on his fore
head had dripped paint
on his nose, pink in
the shape of
glass in a
kaleidoscope

Early Days in the Paddock

the foal sniffs the breath
blown from his nostrils

Barbaro bucked and scampered,
long legs flashing,

slicing the air, back
arched, scatting the breeze

with his long back legs
then curling close

to La Ville Rouge,
exhausted

On the Day of the Longest Light

the foals lean into their
mares under the maples.
Something in the wind
calls to them, lures
them. My Lovely. The
babies doze in the light,
oblivious. They never
dream the world will
move beneath their feet.
Or their bodies could
betray them. For the
moment, they bask in the
warmth of other
bellies, delicate, all legs,
their manes like
school girls' hair,
gleaming and tossed as
what's ahead unrolls
like fringed velvet

On Days Like That

he played in the
grass in butter
cup wind, rolled
on his back. One
woman who
worked with him
says he was
so easy she
could roll him
over and scratch
his belly. It
was before shoes,
before gates
and clockers.
Only the light

on his velvet
body, his mane
becoming the
color of
warm earth

Barbaro and the Other Colts

in the pasture, a
freeze frame, a

caught flash. None of
them move. Not

one snorts. No
light breaks thru

wet bark, the pale
gray still

soundless before
light rips

the mist, before
bucking and leaping,

horses in
silence

steam and glisten

His Mysterious Eye

even at 6 weeks,
soft mahogany,
intelligent. You
could see the sun's
glint, the green

brown sky. Early
June, Barbaro
and five other colts
horse wrestling and
sleeping. Hard play
in the breeze of mint
and clover. A horse
who took to the
halter, a foal nothing
scares, already
running as the
wind was rising
him into the air, the
one you'd look
back at passing

No Wonder Some Grooms Always Spent a Little More Time with Him

he seemed to enjoy people,
let them rub on him. Once
he ripped his leg in the
pasture, developed a splint.
He was stall bound for
two weeks while the farm
staff treated him with cold
hosing and bandages.
There was a mesh door
with a diamond cut out of it
where a horse could put his
head. Even as a baby,
Barbaro liked to keep his
head up. He just liked to
watch things. He was
always like that

On a Day It Seemed the Planets and Stars Chose

Barbaro was weaned,
five months old
with a rope clipped
to his halter. On a
day he was led to a
field without his
mother he called,
whinnied frantically
for her, was too
troubled to eat. His
mare called out
to him, a plaintive
cry. Later the mothers
put their heads down
to lush grass, began
to nibble and
Barbaro did too

Still Un-Named, Known as "La Ville"

he chimed right in
with the program

was always
leader of the yearlings

Especially large for
a late colt, Barbaro

grew in sudden bursts.
When he hit a growth

spurt they were big
growth spurts.

His elbows would
stick out. All of a

sudden he'd stop,
develop out,

look fine again

One Groom's Song

When he was in his stall
you'd walk by him, pat
him on the head and say
"Hey, La Ville, how you
doing?" He just liked

to watch things. He was
a cool horse. It never
bothered him to be
confined to a stall.
That's, the groom said,
"a pretty neat personality"

Bringing Barbaro to Florida

all night the van
twisted thru dark
hills, rumbled
thru three storms.
Horses in darkness.
Some water, some
hay. All night
down thru Kentucky
to Tennessee, to
Georgia. Onyx sky,
scrim of light.
Hours away the
van slithered
under huge oak
trees. Fog hung in

the branches
like the words
"It's here, it's
here," as light
began to out
line branches

Inside the Barn, Clomp of the Yearlings

Photos were taken,
the horse scars and

stars, the horses'
hearts and splashed

colors written
down in a book.

17 months.
If a year in a horse

life equals about 3
years in a human,

Barbaro, all legs,
was like a kid

arriving for his
first day of pre-school

First Yearling Days in Florida

after the dark van ride,
the air wet and sweet
in tangerine wind,
scent of oranges and
lemons, the hard knots,
splints on Barbaro's

front legs kept him in
a stall again. The others
were hand walked,
taken around the pen,
doing figure eights.
Birds he never heard
in Kentucky, fresh
shavings. Waiting for
new bone growth,
waiting for dinner,
waiting to be hand
walked, waiting to be
brushed and for
the sound of
certain voices. He
had waited before,
watched and waited
for dentists, for English,
for Spanish words,
for new water,
fly spray. Learning
to wait, take each day
as it came, as if
he knew he was
learning what could
keep him alive

Those Nights in the Stall

did Barbaro dream
horses galloping?
In the dark, starless,
did he feel the
ground shaking?
Imagine the sound
of hooves on turf?
Was there some
thing in the wind?
The scent of horses

thundering past the
barn, of flying
manes, the beating
of his own heart,
louder than hooves?

When I Think What Her Jockey said About How Easy it was to Take Out Ruffian, I Could Put Barbaro's Name in Instead

so easy in the morning
to take her out and
bring her back. Coming
off the race track, the first
thing she would do was
look for leaves on the
trees, someone to
break off the leaves
for her. She looked all
around, took everything
in. Nothing bothered her:
she didn't have a nerve in
her body. She was
smart. She'd hear a
photographer walking
around and hear the
shutter clicking, raise
her head and look at the
photographer as if
saying go ahead,
take a picture

Moving On to Fair Hill

on his first day
Barbaro got his
name, just before
his second birth

day. No one knew
where he'd take
them, as mysterious
as those van rides
thru the night
or seeing thru fog,
a race track in
mist like
some oval
in heaven

The Sparrows Saw Him

saw his hot heart,
walked under
Maryland maples.
The magnolia
leaves moved when
he moved, his
glossy mane its
own breeze. He
had a love affair
with speed, could
not wait for the
gate to open

A Horse That Transformed You

on him, it was
as if you were
poured on,
were part of
his sailing
over the track
as if he had
wings. A horse
who loves to
run, don't

have to find
the gas pedal on,
only the brakes

On a Horse Like That

you want to dance thru
the night. This horse
makes your wrists
shiver, makes you
bury your face in his
mane. He is the
color of onyx and
velvet, his muscles
under you feel like
part of you, the
electricity of
how you'll rush
thru the blue moon
wild as the white
splotch on his fore
head in this
flight to escape

This Night That the Horse That Can't Be

is waiting under the
open window, a
dream horse moves
thru pomegranates
on a sill. You might
think your wild love
has made him real,
the feel of his
warmth under your
thighs as you
leap, so alive, in
a grove of olives

14

your mouth full
of mane, your
wings his wings,
his withers

When You See a Horse Glistening in the Morning Light

tossing his head,
pawing the earth,
the buttercups and
you see his body
shine, this muscled
colt so recently a
spindly yearling,
trim and firm, a
long legged racing
machine, stunning,
riveting, your heart
catches, fresh, on the
verge of beautiful
and frightening,
and do you think
how from the seed
of so much beauty,
disaster could bloom?

Before the Race

the jockeys in
brilliant colors
walking out in
to the light and
green shade, the
green plants,
green leaves,
water and the
glistening horses

it was as if Barbaro
thought he was playing
a game with a favorite
colt. Think of the first
time he heard a crowd
roar or saw the rainbow
silks of the jockeys
against blue sky. Don't
you want a shot of his
first time in the gate?
How he shook his head,
eyes wide and then the
jockey settles his feet
in the stirrups, the leaves
already tinged with red.
After the bell, Barbaro
exploded in a leap,
cruised, a romp at the
three eighths pole. When
his jockey asked him to
switch leads Barbaro
flattened out. He was an
engine flying in his own
rhythm as if he didn't
know the race was over

And Here Comes Barbaro
(The Kentucky Derby, May 2006)

As Blossoms Rose and Faded

weeks before the
Derby, Barbaro's
days were like
any other, a
stable like
any other

Periwinkle light
behind the spires
at Churchill Downs

On Thursday,
Barbaro breezed.

The night before
the race, his rider rubbed
the colt's forehead

as if he was his child

The Derby

Barbaro, as if
the world was his
coming out of
the barn, strolling,
easy. Someone
says the Derby's
like a wedding,
it goes by so fast.
The chaos, the
energy. Mint juleps
hats, spires,
roses. Horses
at the edge
of simmer

Derby

with Prado in the
saddle, in the
blur of roses
and mint, Barbaro
settled down.
My Old Kentucky
Home, quivering
magnolias. As
the gates sprang
open, Barbaro
stumbled then
was off running.
He was exploding,
then relaxed
his jockey said,
accelerating
and then so
smooth

Only One of Six

to come to the Derby
undefeated. There
in a garden of pastel
hats, hearts and blood
beating, his toe in
dirt, tho Barbaro had
stumbled, struggled
for his stride, now
he was in a sea of
horses, he was
reaching into
himself. He was in a
stalking position.
Suddenly it was as
if he had wings
and was flying over

the track, running
ahead, alone
out in front,
running in love
with running

At the Half Pole

Prado said "I
knew he was
going to be
really tough.
I thought he
was going to
win for sure"
If somebody
beats this
horse today
he grinned "he
is a super
horse, out of
the planet"

Four Golden Hooves Glowing

the turn and
flick of his
ears when he
pulled out
in front. Calm
and glistening,
a Lamborghini,
the engine
hardly used

Barbaro Breathing Fire

The call cruising home,
the wire before them.
They hit it like a wall.
He was floating thru
the sun soaked evening,
thru the music of the
crowd, Prado's hand
on the colt's shoulder

After the Derby

shrieks of
still undefeated.
After Seaborne Chase,
after Stephens
Training Center,
the Keeneland, The
Churchill Breeze
and now The Derby,
the best horse his
assistant trainer
said, the kind of
horse sheiks
dream of

After the Derby

breakfast at Fair Hill.
Everyone wanted a
story about Barbaro.

Before the reporters,
deer and fox ran
in blackness and
Barbaro ate, romped,
ran on the practice

field. The light
was staying longer,
the light was all

Maybe the next
Triple Crown

on everyone's lips

Third Saturday in May
(Just Before the Preakness)

Before His Last Race

Barbaro was out in the paddock
eating grass, being a horse.
"He's used to doing it," his
trainer said. "It doesn't suit
everyone but it suits him."

On the Day of the Preakness

his groom led
Barbaro into a trailer
and then to a stall
with soft deep straw.
In the morning,
brightness, then the
sky turned pewter.
The rain held off.
People were every—
where. Hours later,
Prado pulled on blue,
white and green
racing silks. No
thing felt ordinary

Before the Preakness

Barbaro rolled
and bucked in his
round pen. He
was still growing.
Muscles glistened,
black honey. Life
rooting in the
dark seed of earth.
Sun, pine, wind.
Heartbeats, breath
before the bone

crushing dark day.
if anyone could
have seen ahead
they would have
shut their eyes

Third Saturday in May, The Preakness

the men who spent each day
for months with Barbaro
couldn't hold back their

confidence. "I can't see
him getting beat at all"
one of his trainers said.

The way he strained to
get past every horse
going around the training

track, didn't break a sweat.
Who knows what's possible
and what is not. There

was no way to know
that once Barbaro was
led on to the van under

a passing rain shower,
the horse would never
see the inside of their

barn again

As if Running was Breath
(The Preakness Race)

Day After Day He'd Been Pointing Toward This,

breezed and galloped.
Day after day his jockey
inhaled him. The two
close as lovers. Day
after day, the dream of
jewels, the dark bay
colt's body glistening.
Day after day as cherries
and plum flowers unfurled,
then the hands of maple,
the horse leaped past
as if running was breath

Prado at His Old Stomping Grounds

on the best horse
he'd ever ridden.

Barbaro poised,
eager, playful

looking good,
feeling good,

loading the
gate easily.

The crowd on
fire and then the

latch as the
last horse

loaded and
Barbaro, thinking

it was time
to go

broke thru the gate

Checked, No One

saw anything wrong,
but an ominous sign

if there was a film,
black birds would

hover, flutter
down, two

minutes from
adding to his

legacy, closer
to everything

Dark wings darkening

After He Broke Thru the Gate, Reloaded

Barbaro broke a
step slowly, wasn't
taking the race to
his rivals. he was
always going for
a perfect position.
not this time. He
lagged. "He wasn't
there," his jockey
said, "this isn't
him."

Suddenly the Jockey Felt a

change, a painful
hesitation. Suddenly
he didn't care
about the Preakness,
didn't second guess,
worry about the
Triple Crown. He
stood in the irons and
pulled his struggling
mount out of the
race. Suddenly
Barbaro slowed and
fluttered sideways.
Legs dangling,
Prado slid to the
ground as if he
still felt the shock
waves pulsing thru the
colt's body as the
other horses
galloped on

A Blurred Image

 a horse being
passed by others

a gasp,
then stillness

the light pummeled,
Barbaro struggling

to come to a
halt on 3 legs

he was done
being perfect

A Horse on Three Legs

like a building falling,
a car hanging over
the cliff, not at all
grounded. Onlookers
shudder. Adrenalin
pounding. The day
careens from joy.
"Over" moves thru the
crowd like funeral flowers

As Barbaro Writhed

Prado tried to
hold the horse
still. Vets rushed
with splints,
bandages. *Life
Threatening.*
Stall 40 cleared.
the x ray machine
ready, ambulance
drive geared up.
Racing workers
unfolded a
screen, a make
shift tarp to
keep the horse
from viewers.
"Don't you dare
put this horse
down" a woman
yelled

The Tarp

how everyone knew
what it usually meant

It was spooking the horse.
"Take it down" the

vet said. At the
rail, a woman screamed

Don't, don't, take
the horse home.

Barbaro had a look,
agitated, panicked,

his heart raced,
pulse rate wild,

pupils dilated,
hysterical fright,

but he let the doctor
put the splint on

Loading the Ambulance

Some stood
dazed, vacant

some were sobbing

Some thought there
wasn't a chance

Someone gave Barbaro
a narcotic

Someone steadied him
backed him up the ramp

Someone said they
never saw a

horse so adept at
trying to help those

helping him

A Horse Not Ready for the Barns of Darkness
  Under the Earth

some looked, some
looked away. The
stillness thick and
heavy. The news
spread. Few could
watch any longer. Then
a loud ovation
The ambulance drove
back up the home
stretch with Barbaro
in the back

Barbaro was Still Shaking

still wild to run.

The stillness under a
blazing sky,

silence in the stable
as the big white ambulance

pulled away. It was
quiet, the silence

of the unknown. For
the horse men, the

silence of what they knew

As the Police Escort Followed the Van Over

the wood chip path
Barbaro had walked
like a rock star down
some children took
a piece of poster
board from an old
project, drove
to the closest over—
pass and shivering
in the wind hung
GOD BLESS BARBARO
over the road as
Barbaro stood square
and easy all the way
to New Bolton. Some
said if there'd been
any hay in the hay net
on the ambulance,
Barbaro would have
devoured it. He seemed
to know those touching
him were trying to
help him and he was
going to let them do
what they had to. It
was how he was

While His Life Hung Like Petals in Ice

I think of gymnasts
paralyzed in one
twist, a bullet, a
car careening.
What can change
in an instant.

On the night before
surgery Barbaro
slept a deep sleep.
One doctor said
he was very brave,
well behaved

The lights stayed
on in his trainer's
Fair Hill barn,
slice of yellow
in darkness.

Barbaro's stall
empty under the
moon, the door
slid open as
if he'd return

The Lace of Bones, Tendons, and Ligaments
(Barbaro's Surgery)

Nobody was About to Put This Horse Down
Without Giving Him a Chance to Live

Was the moon rising before
the horse was in his stall,
sedated but hungry? Did the
vet explain "catastrophic" might
not mean the end? Did he show
the "Saving Barbaro" sign
behind the anchor's ear? Did
he tell the horse he turned
down a jet, took US Air out
of West Palm Beach, had a
seat next to the toilet? Did
he tell Barbaro they do things
differently now, no rush
to the hospital? So much stress
and strangeness, how they'd
wait until they really got
it, really knew he had only
three legs to walk on, let
Barbaro figure out how to deal
with it? And did the vet take a
deep breath hearing Barbaro
lie down for two naps that first
night, both for about forty five
minutes, his good limb under
him as night mist hung in
the branches and the sweet
clover dripped with dew?

When He Came To

Barbaro was
put in a sling and
lowered into deep
warm water. He

could gallop, still

half dreaming,
He could wake up
as if swimming

and blindfolded,
he couldn't see he
was lifted by a
pulley suspended

as if flying

The X Rays Looking More Like a Cross Section
of a Bridge Truss

a web of bones criss-
crossed by dark iris,
lines like weathered
leather or wood, you
could imagine this
was not something
once alive but part of
a building. Sirens and
steel, a bone graft
taken from Barbaro's
pelvis. Then, amazing
as a construction site,
the sling where the
drugged horse was
lifted like the side of
a house into a floating
raft. A horse—whale
made for swimming,
something not from this
world, legs in water—
proof tubes as he
might swim home

Though He Almost Jogged Back to His Stall

he's still a coin toss

the surgery
so difficult,

metal implants to
fuse his fetlock

joint, stabilize
the limb to the

point he can
be saved, maybe

a stallion.
A first step.

forget about
when he can

leave, mount
a mare

Because Prado Couldn't Talk About Barbaro
Without Crying

because he wanted to make people
happy, knew everyone wanted
a Triple Crown, wanted a smile
on their face. Because he knew
Barbaro, every time he ran, was
getting better. Because he never
wanted to bring sadness and tears
to people he cared so much about,
his wife, children watching.
The blue sky, the taste of victory.
Because Barbaro looked so perfect

in the post parade, alert and bright,
so anxious he broke thru the
starting gate before it was released.
Because nothing this bad was
imagined, there was for
days no words

Because You've Fallen in Love with What You
Shouldn't

the race track photos
tear you up. In one,
a tiny Prado leans
against the massive
horse, desperate to
keep him from
collapse. In another
someone consoles
the jockey as Barbaro
is taken away. Prado's
whip dangles from
his fingers. His saddle
lies in the dirt beside him

At Night Along the Fields, His Trainer

knows for now the colt is
peaceful in the hospital
stall, a life without pain
would be enough. The
stillness, after the crush of
the Derby, the ambulances,
the dire news. But the
past opens so easily, the
high of two weeks ago, this
floating without a place to
stand. He knows Barbaro is
doing as well as anyone

could hope. Exhaustion is
a drug. "Maybe he will
make it," Matz shudders, half
terrified to even think
that far from this moment.
He pulls one sweet clover
from the earth. It makes him
think of the horse. It
always will

As If Asking "What's Next?"
(June)

Some Nights in Intensive Care at New Bolton Center

the mares nickered,
goats bleated.
New foals made
new foal sounds.
A zoo, a Noah's
ark at midnight,
alpacas and cows,
sheep, pits and
Barbaro, taking
it in

As if He's Asking What's Next

while his 13 X 11 foot stall
was cleaned and new straw
filled it. Barbaro was tied
to one wall. He stayed still,
stared out a 4 panel window.
After a bath, outside his
stall, the cast on his ankle
wrapped in duct tape, he
was led back to where he
rolled twice on his back
in the hay, whinnied a bit,
got up, shook himself off
then went over to the stall
door, as if asking
"what's next?"

When They Put a TV in Barbaro's Stall for the Belmont

the e mails start coming.
They beg the vet not to
let him watch the stakes,
they don't want
him stressed. At post

time, the Derby winner
was alert and staring
intently out of his stall
still looking fit, his
muscles rippling, only
he seemed more
interested in a pregnant
mare about to foal.
And when Jazil crossed
the finish line, Barbaro
was in the back corner
of his stall,
relieving himself

If Barbaro Was to Not Make It

who wouldn't want
to imagine each white
butterfly was something
in him returning, flying,
not bound to the earth
but free as he hasn't been
in the weeks since that
part of his beauty and
speed let him down,
Better than a life
in a stall like a grave
between being alive
and waiting.

In the Hospital Barn at Night

after the last ribbon
of raspberry sky
goes ink and
the food buckets
are still, night
air moves in under

45

the door. A
ventilator hums,
an 11 day colt
gnaws a curtain.
Damp leaves.
night birds. The
plush of dark like
cotton batten around
the alpaca with
a baby that didn't
know how to nurse,
it wraps its velvet
around a young
bull castrated hours
before. Night soothes
the mare with a
high risk pregnancy,
soothes the one
who has just
given birth. In
the soft dark behind
a fence of get well
cards and posters
Barbaro shifts
from leg to leg

So Many Nights in the Barn

Outside, the air's heavy
with thunder and
clover. Curtains a new
foal chewed to ribbons
flutters. A dark filly's
intestinal tract has been
operated on and now
she is starved. The
vet says Barbaro
has been a little
cranky lately,

isn't having much
fun, watches grackles,
birds that can go
anywhere

Sleeping with Horses

even the injured can float
as they once did over
the finish line. In the
vase of the water, the
horses move, their
cappuccino eyes
glistening. To
move with horses
underwater, mysterious
as a slow motion
film. Beads of
water, jewels sparkling
from dark bay flanks
hypnotic as the
water itself. This is a dream
state where the past opens
and the torn old horses
are weightless

You Need a Miracle to Get Through This
(July)

Bad News, Leaking Out Slowly

like an abscess

a new cast, a few new screws.
On Monday, somehow, the unsaid,
a shadow over July

A blacker shade of fear
two days later.
Another cast change

A blip you could
pretend not to notice.
"Abscess." Typical

Still talk of Barbaro being a stud.
Then, up from behind, like a
rapist in an alley

Potential serious complications.
The titanium plate and screws replaced.
The pain meds, the longer time

coming out of anesthesia

feels like a preview

It Took Longer to Recover from Anesthesia from This Latest Procedure

Each statement, code
for nothing going well.
I think of the colt in
film rolling in sweet
grass and buttercups.
The small bad news
comes first like a scout,
a warning. "Small

abscess" before news
of infection. His torn
leg. Two bent screws
before the hardware
was replaced and more
screws added. I think
of other horses, how
everybody tried, of
Barbaro's trainer and
owners, helpless, just
with him in the ICU
stall. How everything
inside them must feel
kicked, how "new
implants and a fresh
bone graft" must terrify

This Rollercoaster to Death, This Hoping, Waiting

Children again send
prayers and flowers.
"Barbaro you are the
first horse I want to
marry." Others beg
to let him run in
green pastures. They
want him to live,
forget about baby
Barbaros. Or at the
worst, a day outside
in the leaves and grass
with other horses,
rump to rump in the
rain, the new air.
Someone says
carbohydrates are
not enough, he needs
the smell of the
outside, grass and

clover. One girl
writes "Please don't
let him stand on
the leg with laminitis"

Laminae

like a tiny forest
of pines, the horse
moving its toes
like a ballerina.
The pine branches
intertwine, each
leg ends in a
single digit. The
canon bone like
a toe nail circling
the toe as that
forest of tiny bones
binds the coffin bone
to the hoof wall.
If the lamina start
to give way, pain
and discomfort.
If enough lamina
detach the coffin
bone rotates with
the hoof or moves
downward and the
pain is too much
to go on

Will the Bones Heal Before the Hardware
    Begins to Loosen?

Will the hoof re-grow?
Will the front legs stay cool?
At dawn, will he stay

bright eyed? Will he sleep
on his side? Does he
miss the crowds,
the cheers? Will he
keep his good spirits?
Does the moon keep him
company? The fillies
with their foals? Does
he hear the tigers,
the lions, watch red
sun rise past hills
clear of the branches
splattering its wild
light over the hospital
barn morning after
morning?

On This Almost Dog Day of August

Camellias still wild with
bees. In shade, green places,
emerald and jade. Another
comfortable night. Light
thru windows in the stall
make Barbaro more
beautiful, ravishing, sun
filtering thru willows,
the way it turns straw in
to gold like Rapunzel

Barbaro's Hoof

it seems a miracle
how from something
so small, twenty
percent of Barbaro's
sick foot, another could
grow mysteriously

as a baby under
skin in the cove of
darkness. Some say
the new hoof will
resemble the hoof it
came from only
slightly, like most
children, never an
exact copy of the cells,
same DNA, the same
blood but, everyone
is hoping, a new hoof
that can stand on its own

Barbaro in the Light, Glistening and Dripping
(August)

Every Time His Trainer Walks into Barbaro's Stall

he feels Barbaro's
eyes looking at him
as if he wants to
do something,
wishes he could
send the horse
out to run. Mist.
His trainer would
lay a blanket of
flowers on Barbaro's
back. Instead, he
measures the
centimeter of
hoof, the horse
asleep in the stall,
changes bandages,
sits in the blackness
still wondering,
sees something in
the horse's eyes
too hard for him
to look at

The First Day Out, Barbaro Grazing

he stood in the air
as if taking in
a new world

just stood,
smelling the air, the grass

He just stood there.
This was a new world

again and his owners couldn't stop beaming

Video of Barbaro in the Grass

hoof sound and the
slow camera pan
from hospital stable
to the paddock. Then,
Barbaro gobbling
and snorting. For a
horse, the doctor says,
grinning, who wants
to be outdoors
there is nothing like it
being outdoors,
nothing like ripping
grass out of the ground

Some Nights Barbaro Dreams

of trails of hard—
wood forests, green
fields as far as any
one could see. In
this dream, nothing
has been torn or
ripped. no part of
his body isn't
perfect. his mane
flows, a dark corn
tassel, mahogany
flag. Nothing isn't
open to him, dirt
road, a wood
chip track, turf the
color of emerald,
miles of cross country
trails ahead and only
the road to ride

Another Barbaro Dream

not, as you might expect,
of the sound of the crowd
after the gate clangs open,
not the flesh, the feel of
earth moving under him.
It's not the roses around
his neck, not his jockey's
leg on his skin or the
photographers moving
toward him like filly—
loves but of a simple
night in his old stall,
the familiar smells, the
night sounds and knowing
his stall mate was near him
and that in the morning
there'd be rhinestones
on grass in the paddock
in early light and his body
could do what it wanted

First Day Out in the Rain

another summer gone

rain pelting maples,
rain to go with hoof music.
Barbaro moving thru mist,
a rain earth opens to,
a sky the color of rain.
Grass smelling of other
ends of summers in the
rain. Wet grass, the washed
wild iris. Barbaro, sparkling
and dripping. Rungs
break on the ladder of
fear in this freeze

frame, this momentary
rain pasture

August, Somewhere Past Sparkling Lakes

as shadows move in
earlier and Barbaro has

been led out, brief outings
to the grassy areas close

to ICU. Somewhere
else, his last stable mate is

being hot walked. Barbaro
is picking his own grass

for the first time in
almost three months. The white

casts and bandages,
color of his splotch and green

green boughs. Dreamers
who imagine Barbaro could race

again remember Red in
Sea Biscuit saying "it's not in his

feet, it's in
his heart"

Against All Odds
(September, October)

When You Start to Feel September in the Air

Barbaro just wants
to roll over in a round
pen, a red tailed
hawk above him.

For a high energy horse,
the stall seems small.
How could he not
long for Fair Hill

On the Metro Slicing October Fog

I think again of the
May Saturday

"Life threatening" on
headline news

Reddening oaks,
echo of the doctor's

answer when asked
"When will you

begin surgery?"
"When you

stop asking me
questions." And then,

the waiting, the
thrill of hearing the

colt practically
jogged back

to his stall, unsure

of what was

ahead, like
now

The Leaf Falling Music

Is Barbaro learning
new music? The sound
of a new gate? Other
voices becoming a
leitmotif morning to
morning the new
blankets, new grass?
Leaves tremble, the
waiting for reports
hums on. Branches
clatter, the unknown,
how a horse can
snow ball fast, how
in a breath, with no
warning everything
can go wrong

Mid-October

Asked "How's he doing,"
the doctor grins, "well,
look at him. You can
see him now. He looks
like a happy horse,
wouldn't you think?"

He's made friends
with a brown Swiss cow,
Mocha, who plods
over once in a
while to nuzzle,

backs off when
she starts to cover
his face with
her tongue

Beyond Us
(November)

Late Fall, Tumbling into Winter

last winter,
Barbaro still
tumbling in chicory,
his belly tickled
grass. Now past
his stall, swans
in a cold pond.
Feathers on the
water. Barbaro's
life, a feather
on water,
flying ahead
scouting the
ponds, still
holding on to
the moons to come

On These Cold Days, November

A new Tao of
bone, strong
tapestry. And
later, new lives,
the idea of
small dark foals

November 20, 2006

Barbaro lying down,
feet forward, eating
the grass Mrs. Jackson
brought. Edgar is
sitting next to Barbaro,
talking to him. "He
loves the horse," she
says, "it's a true

relationship," and Edgar
is smiling that Barbaro
has put on a little
weight, has bright eyes
and was actually
trying to bite him a little

Barbaro, Dawn, Breeders Cup

before it's light,
cats yawn in the
stalls near him,
coil deeper this
first day of frost.
Song of hooves,
lullaby healing.
Anything torn or
broken, a jewel
to guard as the
first color bleeds
thru black air.
Blush streaks
and then
lavender widens.
If horses can read
the wind, can taste
the sounds of
distant mares
galloping on earth,
his heart must
be beating fast

Why Do These Horses Mean So Much?
(December)

Camellias Blooming Thru Warm Winter

earth still not
frozen under
Barbaro's feet.
Overnight who
knows what
could harden.
For now, the
music of
Barbaro's
whinnies, a scarf
of cashmere
like news of
another comfort—
able day. Why
do these
horses mean so much
when we haven't
even met
them?

Because He was Standing There

just standing there looking
like a great horse, his
vet says, just saying he
wanted to go on. It still is
so hard, the worst time
to think about, the
grimmest. It was
crushing. If it hadn't
happened, Barbaro would
be in Kentucky now.
When the Jacksons and
his trainer talked,
when they were discussing
the gravity of what was
going on, there were

no dry eyes. So badly, so
quickly. Only one
individual taking part in
the discussion who didn't
have tears in his eyes:
that was Barbaro
just standing there,
looking great, telling
everyone he wanted to
go on

Before the Moon Rises

deer lie in the
pine groves. Fox
plunge through
frozen reeds.
Plump crows in
the cold trees.
This horse, a
reason to worry,
to hope, to smile.
No snow yet,
this moving past
the last counted
days. If horses
dream of dying,
is it to float
away in
fog or snow?

Grown Lovers of the Black Stallion and Man of War

the ones with paper
horses and statues,
plastic and glass
colts and fillies,
find that lost little

girl again in Barbaro's
eyes. The ones who
didn't believe, now
do believe in miracles
they say. Outside
Barbaro's stall,
"May the Angels of
Healing Continue
to Wrap their Wings
Around you." To
celebrate the horse's
holiday, a custom
made halter,
embroidered blanket,
a Santa hat, even
his own stocking
stuffed with mints,
sugar cubes and hay

Barbaro in December Rain

before it grows colder,
before ice glazes fences
and fox skitter through
dark pines. You might
think Barbaro would
want to go back to his
warm stall but he stands
in the paddock. His
body quivers, darker
muscles glint as the
pale rain falls over
his eyes

No Bandages on Barbaro's Hind

December 13

before the winter trees,
frozen ground. Before
the Equinox and dark
begins to melt, the news
a candle. Healing, healing
and gaining weight.
Before ice skims the
roads at Kennet Square
when the moon sinks,
a half dollar moon,
nothing on his naked leg,
beautiful in its strangeness

In the Last Weeks of Growing Dark, in Earth Too Hard for Barbaro's

hoofglyphs, grapes
wither, even pansies
are ghosts. What
we don't see,
Barbaro's steps,
gingerly, testing.
We don't see
how he
tries earth like a
weanling,
ends his walk
with a firm gait

On the Last Day of the Longest Night

leaf blowers, their
tornado of rusts and
brown gold leaves,

a swirl, like the
news: Barbaro to
leave ICU. Just to
be talking about
it is progress .
Stable, comfortable.
Still, concern, the
icy ground anyone
could crash on.
Still could founder.
The sky pewter.
The vet says never
before had he tried
to save a horse
that had this severe
laminitis. Not yet
out of the woods

On the Day of Least Light

before night's long
sapphire ether, a cold
front moves east and
temperatures cruise
lower down. This dark side
of winter, earth losing
its soft moss rug.
Before ice hooves
could skid on, crack
this last grass, corn
stalk hair blowing
Barbaro hams and
dazzles on TV. His
doctor grins, "he's a
pretty adaptable guy.
he likes to meet other
animals, he really
does, says, what we'd
like to have him meet,

eventually, would be
receptive mares"

Time With Her Slow Spoon

No one
thought he'd make
it this far thru the
times of darkness
except for the
horse with his
"so what, this is
not such a big
deal" look. His
body a different
body than the
beauty he was but
still all Barbaro,
still running
away from
them all

In the Longest Blackness

a wind rises, clatter of
branches, then it is
still. All week,
like the seasons,
change, bloom,
where Barbaro would
be sleeping, where
earth would be
softer than stone
Black sky of
diamonds, black sky
of waiting, the
longer to dream.
Black velvet

wrappings, camouflage
the edges, the new
hoof still an
issue, maybe for
the rest of his life

On the Day Before Light Comes Home, December 21

on the day the falling
fruits have fallen
and mud's glazed
mahogany glass,
those who don't
cry, cry seeing
Barbaro on TV.
The horse, death—
close, the couldn't—
give up horse, this
freak of will, this
hitch in his giddy—
up horse moving,
moving on, with
grace and
brilliance

Winter Solstice

after the warm spell,
the sky looks like
it means business.
Earth cools. Soft
clover that cushioned
Barbaro's feet hardens.
To step off the shore
of the barn, to slog
forward, disaster.
Somewhere else,

maybe blue grass, a
softness, all anyone
could want after
the hard trip to now

The Final Miracle, Fiction
(January)

Before Any Snow

grass stays green.
January. Winter
stirs with a slow
ladle. The cherry
blossoms are
bulging. Barbaro
bored maybe in his
stall of thick
straw and shavings,
this strange winter.
No December or
January smells.
No snow quilt, no
ice jagged as glass.
Wind of mares,
wind of dry leaves.
Barbaro moving
letting go of the past

Record Breaking Warm

when the rain is over,
cherry blossoms open.
Too early, daffodils press
towards the light. Sky, an
a blue oil cloth blue
as the sky the day
Barbaro was born

Brushing Barbaro

first the halter,
then the picking
of his front feet.
Outside, a light
warm rain, a

80

blanket, a shank,
then Barbaro's led
thru the wet pine,
the path a swamp,
branches dripping.
Barbaro grazes
before the curry
comb, before
the body brush,
before the blue
moon, before
what is about
to happen
happens

Before Rain Turns Ice Pellets

Barbaro is covered by
a warm blanket

the last purple
light, last of the

geese flying overhead.
Cold front coming.

A horse lives how many
years if you're lucky?

The smell of warm hair,
horse hair. Those violets

coming under foot,
under earth we

hope will
carry him with ease

Crow Thursday

as pear snow
breaks out across
the pond and the
daffodils with
their own wild
light. If a broken
horse were to
smell the new
earth smells,
mare scent, the
buttercup wind,
sky blue hyacinth
and he was stall
bound and he had
flown over dirt
and grass
suspended and
when birds grazed
the highest
branches and
moths and dragon
flies flocked
thru the air,
would his home
seem a prison?

On the First Day of Snow

images float thru
crystals. White
hands of winter,
images in the
sack of weather.
The jockey's
hand on Barbaro's
neck, the veins.
What's flash

frozen, a quilt
over the frame of
Barbaro eating
golden pears and
spearmint. White
over blue stars.
A day it would be
too cold to go
out anyway. Birds'
snow throats
in the paddock.
Why not this horse
in the wind's breath,
please as white
lace settles over
Lael grass

White Day

not a-pin-back- his-
ears-and-look-at-
you Barbaro day.

Outside snow keeps
on. You can't see
where earth was

scarred. Not a wildly
nipping, doing what
horses do day,

there's a stillness, a
no nickering white.
It's a lying down

in the afternoon to wake
up to fog day, to a
Monday full of

cold flowers

Almost Half a Year Since the Bad News of Laminitis

Barbaro, looking like
a statue

Still, unease.
Does it have a

shape, a color?
Ducks on the pond,

heron. Something
unsettled, a

feeling. Is it
tender? Unbreakable?

Cardinals swoop for
crumbs as Barbaro

grazes. Light
streams on his four hooves

Still not out of the woods

When He Stepped to the Door

when he showed his
owner something, that
it was not alright.
Something, the glint
gone in his eyes,
the way he walked.
It was how she could
tell something wasn't
as it had been days
before. the first "ok"
about his condition, a
warning. There were

no stars, no moon. Just
Barbaro standing in
the door, what we
don't know
shadowing him

He Is Getting Up and Down on His Own

All day, in and out
of blurred shadows,
a Sunday no one
could settle on
anything, fell
into darkness.
Barbaro rested in
his stall while
the world waited
for an update.
A new hoof
wall, the many
months to grow it.
The torn lamina,
tissue binding the
hoof to the foot.
"Grow Hoof Grow"
hanging on the fence,
the moon and hazy
stars rising and
falling in their
accustomed places

On the Last Weekend

someone wants to
send out ribbons to
Barbaro, sapphire
or crimson, ribbons
of silk, of velvet or

maroon satin, maybe
japonica lace. Some
want to let them flow
over rivers and plains,
deserts and snow
like those steamers
immigrants, heading
to a new country,
tied to the ones left
on shore as if to hold
on to what they loved
but couldn't keep

To Write a Book about Barbaro before January 29

when you don't know the end

how do you finish?
A badly torn horse

in love with life.
You can't imagine

he won't win, he
always has.

The horse lies down
in our heart,

you have to believe
he'll make it

even knowing
the odds, even with
a miracle after
a miracle, a story

suspended as
Barbaro was on the

track, still, the
final miracle,

fiction

How Many Times Can One Get Punched in the
        Face and Still Continue

Michael Matz

on the grayest Sunday,
in the colorless ice
studded wind, how
did talk of Barbaro
being able to leave
the hospital the
doctors saying
horses that live as
long as Barbaro
get to go home
become suddenly
so far from when he
was free to run and
feel soft grass beneath
healthy feet?

On This Dark Sunday

January 28

A woman is standing
in her home office.
It's so cold and
there's hardly any
light left. The
light's getting
dim in the house
but she notices

for the last hour
there has been a
single beam of sun
light shining thru
the closed blinds,
spilling a brilliant
beam thru stained
glass on to the
Barbaro statue and
photograph. It is
the only sun beam
in the room and
it has not moved

Even the Last Morning

even when the vet
said he was worried,
said upset, couldn't
sleep, something
the way Barbaro had
always rallied, the
old mantra, the
old minor key an-
other crisis coda.
How the horse, how
those who loved
over came so much,
already in the
past tense

Most of the Time He was Happy

his vet says,

ate some grass
for breakfast Monday morning

was tranquilized,
then a slight overdose

of anesthesia. It
couldn't have been more

peaceful he
said fighting tears.

"People love greatness,
people love the

story of his bravery"

He was different, a
different horse

The last night it
was different. "It was more

than we wanted
to put him through"

Beyond Pain
(Barbaro's Death)

We Don't Choose, It Chooses Us

the night before,
some talked to their
horses, some held
their breath. Some
remembered how
they watched
surgeries, waited
for recovery. Some
thought of
wounded mares,
premature foals,
how it was
touch and go.
Some were
praying, some
were already
weeping

On That Day

some cried at their desks
at the news,

watched for falling stars.
Some smiled at apples,

carrots, pears, his
favorite things,

try to believe
Barbaro now is

beyond pain,
healed, running

with Ruffian and Secretariat

Hearing the News

people driving
can barely see
the road. Already
he is buried
in their hearts.
Some leave offices
to weep. A horse can
never tell you his
last words but
the children
know them,
wanted to tie
notes to Barbaro
and fly them
up to heaven

On the Night of Barbaro's Death

some find it hard
to shut down their
computer as if
this makes it more
final, turning it
off and going to
sleep. Others find
comfort in shots
of Barbaro in the
grass showing
off with Dr. Dean,
shooing flies with
his casted leg or
nuzzling Mocha
the cow or warily
eyeing a small cat

Others on the Last Night Think Of

small miracles,
how Barbaro stood
as the wind shifted
in the brightest
December light
thru windows he
watched for those
who came daily,
how he must have
known he was loved

For Dr Richardson, Those Other Mornings

his first stop,
Barbaro's stall,
his first thought,
early light on
the blue bowl
near his coffee
as the white moon
rose, was Barbaro.
It would have been
Barbaro on the
evening of the
last counted days,
It was the first
thought on the
first day of morning
rounds without
him, the morning
empty, the rounds
empty as his
stall

On the Second Day after Barbaro's Death

Matz keeps working,
hardest to think and
talk about the horse,
better to keep going

he hasn't slept in
months somebody
says. Two cars out
side the barn. "Go

Barbaro" on the
bumper. In the tack
room a pair of
bouquets on his

desk, a copy of
Wednesday's Daily
Racing Form with
Barbaro's obit

on the cover and
above it and to the
right of the desk,
Barbaro crossing

the wire at the
Derby, four
feet off
the ground

The Nights After Some Scrolled Blogs Like They Did Everyday, as if The Death Could Not Be Real

I had a premonition
a friend writes,
there was a man in
front of me in

military dress,
long black coat,
black beret. He
took his hat
off and was
beating it
against the
counter. I saw
there was hair all
over it. Horse hair.
He smiled and
my friend said he
must be one who
helps board the caissons
for military funerals.
How he got hair
on him I'm not sure
but I can imagine when
he heard about Barbaro
he must have gone
to his horses
and nuzzled
them

A Horse Can Never Tell You His Dreams

but you can see
freeness when he
rears and bucks.
A horse can live
until 20 or 30
if luck lives in
his bones. When
he is in your
heart you don't
own him, he's
like the snow or
the leaves with
their own laws.

Not even his
owners own him.
Glint in his mane,
how he flew
over air, 4
feet above
incandescent as
earth moved under him

Someone Says Some Horses

know, have an
inner knowing,
something inside
say on the night
before a race.
they have a
sense when it
is time to leave,
accept it with
grace, go from
flesh to dust
in fields with
out fences as if
whispering to the
horses you
can't hear
whinnying
to them,
beckoning

The Sad Songs Haunt the Longest
(Barbaro: Beyond Brokenness)

Weeks After the Eclipse Awards

one voter who
gave Barbaro his
vote said it will
be really hard to
sit in a movie
theater with his
grandkids some
day watching a
movie about the
life of Barbaro and
try to explain
why he wasn't
horse of the year
or remember the
horse that won

As the Forced Wild Plum Opens

and light stays longer,
as Derby Saturday
rushes up, Barbaro's
vet mends tissue and bone.
Some things heal so
slowly. The night air of
almost too sweet tangerine,
the cat in the sun. The
sound of the gate in
each race makes one ache.
No one knows what
will come. Music in a
minor key drifts back over
black pines. The sad
love songs haunt the longest

Barbaro Is No Longer in His Stall in New Bolton

That stall was too
small for his spirit. He
gallops freely among
us. He is in the snow
crystals somebody
says, it's his hooves
when it thunders. He
is no longer stall
bound. He is in the
wind, in the rain, in
the buttercups he loved

Watching Barbaro's Siblings

tearing thru new grass,

full brothers. The
long shadow over

Churchill Downs
this year isn't

the spires, it's
Barbaro in the

orange blossoms,
in the dripping

mint leaves,
in each torn bloom

rising and falling

Days Before What Would Have Been Barbaro's Fourth Birthday

I think of the
gold pears for
him, color of
sun, the best
because he was.
And then, of
his first night,
how he slid,
followed the
curve of his
mother's womb,
her body into
soft straw.
Later a groom
whispered to
him calmly in
Spanish, words
I can't translate
as I can't this
place where he
isn't months
later, his ghost
a hole inside

Then, Finally, the Twin Spires

mist in silver.
The parade to the post.

Weep no more
in our blood

where the horse
with wings, pink

saddle cloth and the
blue green silk

haunts more wildly
when the dogwood returns

Looking at Barbaro's Full Brother

long legs,
the white up
them as if
dipped in
snow or
flowers.
Pale swatch,
a high mover
like Barbaro
stepping high
after the Derby.
The newborn
sleeps in the
frost. When
the trainer
came La Ville
Rouge moved
to the front,
hovered over
her baby,
"you can see'"
some one says,
"Barbaro's
shoulder"

Barbaro's Birth Stall. Empty

no one can bear
another horse
in this stall.
Stony silence,
cold rising up,
the stall with its

diamond shaped
opening
Let it rest

Body by Da Vinci

his beauty, his
speed, but more,
it was Barbaro's
spirit, contagious,
how it captured
crowds. Sick and
injured people
said they were
glued to how he
would not quit,
fought so hard,
his fights becoming
their fights. For a
while, in a race
with a champion,
they were
champions too

When Sir Thomas Browne Said

Life is pure flame and we live by an invisible sun within us

I think of the light
in Barbaro's eyes,
the "whatever,
whatever." His
grace, his burning,
even in uncertainty,
nickering at fillies,
a flicker for the
mares, the green
Lael grass, the

summer air he felt
good enough to
rear in

In the End, Barbaro Eclipsed All the Others

hardened horsemen
said he was majestic
as any animal
they'd ever seen,

that they never
saw a horse that
looked the way
Barbaro did.

A coiled spring,
eyes burning, his
coat a blaze. He
was raging to

run. In the
Derby, taking
control in the final
turn as fatigue

overwhelmed the
others, almost
playing as if
Barbaro made the

far turn outside
so he could see his
owners and they
could see him

To Hold On

greatness walks
hand to hand
with grief. It's
the way beauty,
greatness, dissolve,
are ephemeral,
part of the price,
this essence
that makes
it so hard
to lose

From the Author

"Grief is the price we pay for love," Queen Elizabeth said at a New York remembrance service for those lost in the September 11th tragedy, a phrase she used at different somber events. It was echoed eloquently by Gretchen Jackson the day of Barbaro's death when Melissa Kula quoted the Queen's words to her. It is still our mantra. In so many, a Barbaro shaped hole. Some have worked to transform grief and loss into work to help all horses in Barbaro's memory. Many are working to end laminitis, end horse slaughter and to rescue and care for threatened horses whose foals already are named in Barbaro's honor. Many have been deeply changed by Barbaro, have called this "the Barbaro effect." When I was desperately looking for an issue of *Blood Horse* I couldn't find, another woman who loved Barbaro, a stranger, was compelled to find it for me and send it. Because of Barbaro.

From the first race I saw him dazzle in, "Barbeero" as they mispronounced it, had something mysteriously engaging about him. Who knows why we fall so deeply in love with anybody, a horse. For me, a non-horse person until Ruffian grabbed my heart, Barbaro has become part of my every day.

I want to thank so many: Laura Boss, Alice Pero, Laura Chester and Jordan for reading the manuscript and for their support. I didn't plan to write this book. One poem that May and that would be it. But the months since have been shaped by Barbaro. From the wonder and joy of his May 6th Kentucky Derby win, to the terrible periods following the Preakness, I listened for reports on Google and then Tim Wooley's site with updates from Alex Brown as I traveled from Virginia to Canada, California, New York, Vermont. I owe so much to the shared stories and information on that site and others (there were so many posts from countless Fans of Barbaro, I know I will leave some who wrote beautifully out inadvertently but I think of Harriette, Jonna, Chris B., Laurie H, Martina, Lee, Dora, Lou Ann, Cheryl J and so many others as well as a story from my friend Ginny), to the videos and films, reports, articles, clips from Barbaro's early days to the end. The stories and words of Barbaro's connections, his owners Roy and Gretchen Jackson, Bill Sanborn and Barbaro's grooms and stable help, trainer Michael Matz and Peter Brette, his jockey Edgar Prado and his surgeon after the Preakness, the amazing Dr. Dean Richardson, have entered our psyche, and entangled in our consciousness.